HARBINGER A

EDITOR-IN-CHIEF: Dustin Pickering
ASSISTANT EDITORS: Z. M. Wise
                       Stuti Shree
Honcho of 1,000 Words: Alex Maass

Contact Dustin Pickering for submissions:
Editor@transcendentzeropress.org

Twitter: @TZPress1

HARBINGER ASYLUM is a quarterly journal for literature and the arts.

Printed in the United States of America

ISSN: 2644-2221
ISBN: 9798596047219

Cover illustration by Vera Ikon
Cover design by Vera Ikon

You can find us at www.transcendentzeropress.org
"Like" us on Facebook! It's an ego thing.

You never know what you will find inside...

HARBINGER ASYLUM!

2020-Early 2021, or
How I Learned to (Never) Stop Worrying and
"Love" Global Anxiety

"I don't know where I'm going from here, but I promise it won't be boring!" Before this commences any further, I would like to be selfish for a brief moment and set aside a few words for David Bowie. Earlier this month marked the fifth year of his absence from this planet, as well as what would have been his seventy-fourth birthday. We have lost many artists in many respected fields over the years, including Gil Scott-Heron, Leonard Cohen, Selena, Prince, Greg Lake, and countless others. David Bowie meant and still means a great deal to me as a creator, as well as a human being. The bounty of work and tremendous impact he left behind for his musical contemporaries and his descendants cannot be unmatched. Furthermore, and I hate to seem melodramatic, but if it was not for David Bowie's words and aural pleasures, I would not be on Earth, existing in this physical life. Around the middle of my sophomore year of high school, I was ready to take my own life. By some stroke of luck, Bowie's music was able to reach me at a time when friends and family could not. My inner voice heard the dulcet tones, became encircled by musical wonderment, and whispered to me, "You are *not* finished yet." I owe him an infinite amount of gratitude for many silent gestures, including: introducing me to a number of gifted artists from around the globe, helping me to embrace the full power of diversity and eclectic nature within the arts, and breathe new life in me. This newfound breath of life added a dash of a unique sense of being, as well as a sense of self. David, wherever you are in the Cosmos, 'thank you' would be an understatement. As Scott Walker said to you on your fiftieth birthday, "I'll have a drink to you…on the other side of midnight."

Until last Wednesday, a small boy isolated himself in a toy store the size of a mansion. He remained as cloistered as humanly possible. His mother insisted that they leave and that he could not have the toy he so desperately desired. His mother tried every tactic that her parental skills could manifest, but to no avail. It was useless. The boy simply refused to leave. This situation was the only analogy I could concoct to describe D****d T***p, the former President of the United States. So much is to be said about the 'actions' within his presidency, the lack of tact he blatantly showed, as well as the pomposity of his overall demeanor. My father gave the best description of T***p. He said, "He is a caricature of himself." Even repeating that remark aloud brings me to tears induced by hysterical laughter. The truth is evident, as well as being stranger than fiction. It is worth noting that while I am unashamedly writing this way about the jive turkey that slightly over half of the country voted for, I am by no means glorifying the opposition, either. I daren't bring up my explicit political views as an individual to the table, mainly because they are beyond jaded to begin with. While I have issues that I stand for and against, I see no reason for them to reach the public eye when the very country I reside in is more divided than united in more ways than one. I have not sided with either major party since I can remember, but I contribute as a citizen in any way possible. An individual votes with their heart, their mind, and their gut instinct. If and when we become more united, I may feel more inclined to discuss said views.

Like numerous other political skeptics, I will be watching in the wings to see how this newfangled presidency unfolds. Whatever ensues, I am thankful that the T***p has officially left the building. After the insurrection, there was absolutely nothing that could salvage his title…not after every insignificant syllable that was uttered from his lips. I am almost envious of textbook writers and young schoolchildren in the sense that this particular chapter of American and world history will be taught in such a way that will never be forgotten. In addition to being an insult to the country, the name (and word) T***p will permanently instill terror into the hearts of many, as well as secretive and public elation for others. It was a horror comedy film with so many sequels that it became an internationally known franchise. I demand a refund for the loss of my brain cells. There is one beautifying factor of T***p's brief tenure as president, one that I will miss for as long as I live: the bottomless pit of free entertainment, as well as the entertainment value that followed. From the endless piles of memes and song parodies to the talented people who can impersonate him and his arsenal of mannerisms, wit knows no end. Fun fact: T***p was the only president who blocked people on Twitter. I am quite jealous of the few people I know who have earned that badge of honor. Then again, Twitter bestowed an even *bigger* honor on the Chief Blocker himself. Oh, digital glory! May this new chapter unify us in boundless fits of laughter. I also feel the need to remind you that everything displayed is merely my opinion. My words are not gospel, despite the outrage nation we live in where the attitude of one too many individuals is, "Everyone is entitled to *my* opinion, and your belief system is lower than dust."

After viewing the inauguration and the host of multifaceted artists who received the *genuine* honor of performing before Joe Biden, Kamala Harris (First Woman and First POC Vice President…absolutely incredamazing), their diverse team, and the entire nation, one person's distinctive performance stuck with me. It was not Jennifer Lopez. It was not Lady Gaga. It was none other than Amanda Gorman, the youngest National Youth Poet Laureate and the youngest poet to recite at an inauguration. I regret to say that prior to this reading, I have only heard her name being spoken during conversations about my literary contemporaries. After watching selected recitations and reading certain compositions, her piece 'The Hill We Climb' sent my cranium and third eye for a loop. Not only was her voice full of conviction and soul, but the words she expelled screamed truths we longed to hear. From moments of her history to the current state of affairs, 'The Hill We Climb' is the epitome and living embodiment of human sensibility, a wakeup call that not only belongs to this country, but the entire blue-green globe that we inhabit. We are but mere guests in this living, breathing sphere and it is our duty to preserve it beyond our abilities. After all, as the old adage goes, "The Earth does not belong to us. We belong to the Earth." Amanda Gorman's honor as an inaugural poet stems from a prestigious role that only a small handful of other have played. They are as follows: Robert Frost, Maya Angelou, Miller Williams, Elizabeth Alexander, and most recently, Richard Blanco. Besides the usual set of messages, musical performances, praise, and other inauguration rituals, the poem is said to exemplify who we are as a country and the actions we *should* be taking. It is a gentle, yet harsh reminder of the matters that are and the matters that will be. In this century, 'The Hill We Climb' is nothing short of needed, the jolt of electricity to shock us back to life after everything we have endured thus far. In addition to the multitude of medical staff members and frontline workers receiving the vaccines they so rightfully earned, Amanda Gorman is a hero in my book. How she recited her piece will forever be ingrained in my mind. May this excerpt from her poem affect you the same way, Dearest Readers.

"But, one thing is certain,
if we merge mercy with might,
and might with right,
then love becomes our legacy
and change our children's birthright."

Z. M. Wise

January 21-23, 2021

CONTENTS

BIOGRAPHIES

Sudip Chattopadhyay was born in 1979 in West Bengal, India. He has authored six books of poems:*'Jekhane Bhramanrekha'* (Where the Peregrinated Line is) in 2009, *'Alphatone'* in 2016,*'Mujrimpur'* (The Land of Convicts) in 2016,*'Shamibriksher Niche'* (Under the Shami Tree) in 2018,*'Aharlipi'* (Feeding inscription) in 2018 and *'Eklami'* (Affinity with Solitude) in 2020. By profession, he is an assistant teacher in a Govt. institution

John Jack *Jackie* (Edward) Cooper is the creator of *These Are Aphorithms* (http://aphorithms.blogspot.com), author of *Ten* (Poets Wear Prada, 2012),*Ten ... more* (Poets Wear Prada, 2016), and translator of *Wax Women* by Jean-Pierre Lemesle (International Art Office: Paris, 1985). His work has appeared widely, in print and online, most recently in *The Opiate*, *Paris Lit Up 7*, *Brief Wilderness*, *Jerry Jazz Musician*, and *The National Beat Poetry Anthology 2020*; forthcoming in *Paris Lit Up 8* and the *Blue River Review*. He is Editor and Co-Publisher of Poets Wear Prada, a small press based in Hoboken, New Jersey. A graduate of the University of Pennsylvania, he lives in Paris.

Robin Wyatt Dunn was born in Wyoming in 1979. You can read more of his work at www.robindunn.com

J. H. Johns "grew up and came of age" while living in East Tennessee and Middle Georgia. Specifically, the two places "responsible" for the writer that he has become are Knoxville, Tennessee and Milledgeville, Georgia. Since then, he has moved on to Chicago- for a brief stint- and New York City- for a significantly longer stay. Currently, he is "holed up" in a small town where when he is not writing, he tends to his "nature preserve" and his "back forty." His goal is to surround his house with all sorts of vegetation so as to obscure it from the gaze of the "locals." He is assisted in this task by his coonhound buddy and companion, Roma. J. H. Johns was a Pushcart nominee in 2018.

John Bowden is a retired high school English teacher and administrator. He lives in Haddon Heights, NJ, with his husband, Russell, and their assortment of Covid gloves, masks and bleaches.

Anwesha Paul is a UX designer and graphic artist from Kolkata, India who is also into writing, having published several pieces in various print and online publications. Anwesha is an animation filmmaker whose short films have been screened and awarded in various national and international film festivals.

Ajanta Paul is a widely-published poet, short story writer and critic from Kolkata, India who has been in academia for ages and has returned to her first love - writing. She did her PhD in English from Jadavpur University in the 1990s and is currently working at Women's Christian College, Kolkata. She is a Pushcart nominee who has published her poems and short stories in various reputed Indian, American and Canadian online literary journals in addition to print media including *The Statesman*, *The Telegraph Colour Magazine*, *The Economic Times* and *Youth Times*. Dr. Paul's poems have appeared in various national and international anthologies of poetry.

Nicholas Karavatos is a lecturer in poetics at the Arab American University of Palestine near Jenin in the West Bank. He was a U.S. Ambassador's Distinguished Scholar to Ethiopia in 2018 at Bahir Dar University, and from 2006 through 2017, an assistant professor of creative writing at the American University of Sharjah in the United Arab Emirates. He is a graduate of Humboldt State University in Arcata and New College of California in San Francisco. Of his 2009 book *No Asylum*, David Meltzer writes: "Nicholas Karavatos is a poet of great range and clarity. This book is an amazing collectanea of smart sharp political poetry in tandem with astute and tender love lyrics. All of it voiced with an impressive singularity." Kevin Killian writes: "Nicholas Karavatos points out that there is 'no asylum' anywhere, in a figurative sense, because even the parts of the world in most opposition to each other are bound up seamlessly in a net of shared reference, sensual pleasure, and invasive, sometimes assertive media. And misunderstanding. He is a prophet as well as a poet—maybe the canary we've sent down the coal-mine."

Gavin Bourke grew up, in the suburb of Tallaght, in West Dublin. Married to Annemarie, living in County Meath, he holds a B.A. in Humanities, from Dublin City University, an M.A. Degree, in Modern Drama Studies and a Higher Diploma in Information Studies, from University College Dublin. His work broadly covers, nature, time, memory, addiction, mental health, human relationships, the inner and outer life, creating meaning and purpose, politics, contemporary and historical social issues, injustice, the human situation, power and its abuse, absurdism, existentialisms, human psychology and behaviour, truth and deception, the sociological imagination, illness, socio-economics, disability, inclusivity, human life, selfishness and its consequences, as well as urban and rural life, personal autonomy, ethics, grand schemes and the technological life, in English and to a lesser extent, in the Irish Language.

Lynn White lives in north Wales. Her work is influenced by issues of social justice and events, places and people she has known or imagined. She is especially interested in exploring the boundaries of dream, fantasy and reality. She was shortlisted in the Theatre Cloud 'War Poetry for Today' competition and has been nominated for a Pushcart Prize and a Rhysling Award. Her poetry has appeared in many publications including: Apogee, Firewords, Capsule Stories, Gyroscope Review and So It Goes. Find Lynn at: https://lynnwhitepoetry.blogspot.com and https://www.facebook.com/Lynn-White-Poetry-1603675983213077/

Dharmpal Mahendra Jain was born (1952) and raised in tribal reserve of Jhabua, India. **Dharm** is a Toronto based Author. He writes in Hindi and has five published books- three collections of satirical essays and two collections of Poetry. He is a columnist for two prestigious journals *Chankya Varta* and *Setu*. His works have appeared in prestigious Hindi journals across the world.

E. Martin Pedersen, originally from San Francisco, has lived for 40 years in eastern Sicily where he taught English at the local university. His poetry has appeared most recently in Soundings East, Vox Poetica, LitBreak, Muddy River Poetry Review and Slab. Martin is an alumnus of the Squaw Valley Community of Writers. His collection of haiku, *Bitter Pills*, has just come out. His poetry chapbook, *Exile's Choice*, is scheduled for publication by Kelsay Books, as is his collection, *Method and Madness*, by Odyssey Press. Martin blogs at: https://emartinpedersenwriter.blogspot.com

Self-identifying as a neurodiverse, two-spirit, elder storyteller with deep Pacific Northwest roots, **Lindsey Morrison Grant** attributes successful recoveries and wellness regimen to an invaluable support network, personal accountability, meditation practice. ..... and creative expression in words, sounds, and images.

Reena R. is from India but lives presently in Sharjah . She is the recipient of the Reuel Prize for Poetry 2018. She has co- edited two anthologies and is a practicing poet.

Mrs. Navneet K Maun was born in Kanchrapara, West Bengal. Did her initial schooling from Oak Grove School, Jharipani, Mussoorie. She furthered her education from Regional College of Education, Bhubaneshwar. She did her Graduation and BEd from there. She did her Masters in English Literature from Banaras Hindu University, Varanasi. She has vast experience in teaching and has retired as a Senior Teacher from a Public School in Delhi. Her hobbies include reading, travelling, writing and cooking.

Belinda Subraman has been writing poetry since the 6th grade and publishing since college. She had a ten year run editing and publishing Gypsy Literary Magazine 1984-1994. She edited books by Vergin' Press, among them: Henry Miller and My Big Sur Days by Judson Crews. She also published Sanctuary Tape Series (1983-89) which was a mastered compilation of audio poetry and original music from around the world. She's been published in 100s of magazines, printed and online, academic and small presses. She has a Master of Arts from California State University. Her archives are housed at University of New Mexico, Albuquerque. Her latest book is Left Hand Dharma from Unlikely Books, 2018.
In 2020 Belinda began an online show called GAS: Poetry, Art &Music which features interviews, readings, performances and art show in a video format available free at http://youtube.com/BelindaSubraman Belinda is also a mixed media artist. Her art has been featured in Unlikely Stories, Eclectica, North of Oxford, El Paso News, Red Fez and Raw Art Review. She sells prints of her work in her Mystical House Etsy shop: https://www.etsy.com/shop/MysticalHouse?ref=seller-platform-mcnav

Stephen Bett is a widely and internationally published Canadian poet with 24 books in print. His personal papers are archived in the "Contemporary Literature Collection" at Simon Fraser University. His website is stephenbett.com

A. Whittenberg is a Philadelphia native who has a global perspective. If she wasn't an author she'd be a private detective or a jazz singer. She loves reading about history and true crime. Her other novels include *Sweet Thang, Hollywood and Maine, Life is Fine, Tutored* and *The Sane Asylum.*

Dr. Paramita Mukherjee Mullick has transformed to a poet from a scientist for the sheer love of poetry. She has published six books and her poems have been widely published in India and in international journals. She is the Founder President of the Intercultural Poetry and Performance Library Mumbai Chapter. Some of her poems have been translated into 36 languages. She has been blessed with awards like the Poetess of Elegance 2019, Nobel Lauraete Rabindranath Tagore award and many more. She received the Gold Rose from MS Productions , Buenos Aires, Argentina for promotion of literature and culture.

Sanket Mhatre is a well-known bilingual poet writing in English & Marathi. He has curated Crossover Poems – a multilingual poetry recitation sessions that unifies poets from different languages on a single platform. Apart from this, Sanket Mhatre has been invited to read at Kala Ghoda Arts Festival, Poets Translating Poets, Goa Arts & Literature Festival, Jaipur Literature Festival, Vagdevi Litfest and Akhil Bharatiya Marathi Sahitya Sammelan. Besides curation & recitation, Sanket Mhatre has also created Kavita Café – a Youtube Channel that combines cinematic vision with visual poetry. He's also a columnist who contributes regularly to leading news daily in India.

Paul Ilechko is the author of three chapbooks, most recently "Pain Sections" (Alien Buddha Press). His work has appeared in a variety of journals, including Juxtaprose, Rogue Agent, Cathexis Northwest Press, Thin Air Magazine and Pithead Chapel. He lives with his partner in Lambertville, NJ.

Sunil Sharma is a Mumbai-based senior academic, critic, literary editor and author with 22 published books: Seven collections of poetry; three of short fiction; one novel; a critical study of the novel, and, nine joint anthologies on prose, poetry and criticism, and, one joint poetry collection. He is a recipient of the UK-based Destiny Poets' inaugural Poet of the Year award---2012. His poems were published in the prestigious UN project: Happiness: The Delight-Tree: An Anthology of Contemporary International Poetry, in the year 2015. Sunil edits the English section of the monthly bilingual journal *Setu* published from Pittsburgh, USA.

ONLY AND AGAIN by DUSTIN PICKERING

Illustrations by Sufia Khatoon

published by SETU PUBLICATIONS

available soon on Amazon.com

With Love as the Muse, the poet struggles within eternal realms of question. His doubts fuel his love of Creation and he accepts the burden of the eternal recurrence. The mystery puzzles and defines him as he scrapes through all relevant philosophical trajectories. Finally he recognizes that the fruit of philosophy is rotting on its vine—*metaphysics is dead*!

These poems are dedicated to real people whose value to the poet is immeasurably without reconciliation to the world of appearance.

This collection ponders and pontificates the age-old questions; strangely, it does not prepare answers but riddles the Unground.

Aethereal Days

Sudip Chattopadhyay

1.

Maroon coloured silence, I have seen you
                    On a mundane evening
Walking towards an anaemic confusion, Monday intertwined in your fingers

Wind is lying down on the streets crouching its wings
Only the flames of blood, leaving this scene, have entered the clouds

When I opened my shirt after returning and a button dropped off
Who-knows-who appeared and stitched my eyes with fine threads of water

Since then in every dream I see
A button dropping off, a button getting tired
                    A button falling asleep all alone

2.

Where should I bury the shadows of our consolation

Though that reposed lash bespeaks of your hair
As well as of the annoying winters and the wingless cold-creams

Why didn't you save those funny and comic films
Why did you wipe the imaginary characters off your eyes

So are you searching to collect sharp satires by saving gestural winks
                    Having kept white frost on both sides of memory?

Slightly stirring the shadow of consolation before and after every murder

3.

I have never worn an olive-crown. Though in those days
An entire stadium used to be inside your head, and
Who-knows-who placed a race of longing within me

Whistling was produced by exudation of air
And how I used to touch the shadows of April spectatorless
Colourful woolen December! Until you found out
The brown mask, the chorus-clapping

And picking up the sleeping rabbit from the fable
                         We named it Etiquette

4.

The round-shaped zero is oscillating
As if anguish would be torn down if greed is hung on it
Surpassing our rebirth this zero is attainable

I blow my life, it rolls on towards twilight
                         Thorns of sin prick
Will then the veil of existence blast

I contemplate, how memory can be regained
How shall I spread over past deeds
                The carpet of mercy and pity

5.

Schemed sarcasm, our mellifluous elocution is weltering at your feet
Who will pull it up in the overwhelming land of cottons, nurse the fresh wounds

With the stories of water and blades the morning news gets sharpened everyday
And that yellow bus, customarily, carries away our daily rumours

Schemed sarcasm, wrapping the darkness within handkerchiefs, our mellifluous elocution
                         Has not yet learnt any such slogan till date

6.

Our Bengali language is in deep slumber among the foreign tales
                              I can never wake her up

Separating the doubled syllables I relax her breath
Replacing the sharp punctuations I conserve the indigenous rituals of our language

The Bengali language budges, changes her posture in sleep
I watch, the seven deadly sins sitting amidst her hair in a circular shape
And primitive idioms oozing down from her forehead with massive verbs

7.

Coming to watch a movie, at the very outset, you are trying to comprehend what you don't
want to watch
Peeping into the movie you wish to witness the future

The threads of the story are getting lost in every ten minutes
Only thing to do now --- is to rely on instinctive tendencies

Every frame that has taught you to be different
Is actually a battle against each and all predestined doom ---
Will you ever bow down to such fantasies?
When laughter is erupting out from feet and the tongue gradually getting lengthened
                              Is suffocating your throat

Coming to watch a movie, at the very outset, you are trying to comprehend an ocean
Peeping into the movie you wish to witness
                              If it too has any thirst

8.

Why do you sell colourful balloons on such a rainy day
The afternoon that hasn't tumbled down till today
            At its feet there are a few insignificant pebbles and tiny glass-globules

Your supple leisure is resting in solitude amidst some vegetation-society

Adventitious prop-roots are coming down, adventitious prop-roots of soul coming
down constantly

On such a rainy day you look like a school-returned sunset

9.
I have rolled up curiosity

Peeling layer by layer darkness behold that stag
The striped lake near his fear

So shall we pick up liberating our thirst our old syllabus
                Thrown-away cover of timid elegance?

Separation of friendships hovering

Emancipating the glories of past journeys I experience
That our conjugal life is clandestine in a country of black curtains

10.
You are undressing the costume of dream
Foreign alphabets are intruding breaking our myths

You are pulling up sleep from the canyon
Your nerves are on high-alert at the pulley

Someone from the incomplete novel
Is rubbing and deleting our first kiss

Translated by the author and edited with Nilotpol Roy

Lot, Again Unrequited

John Jack Cooper

The woman I love turns my heart to stone.
Her ebullient curls tender more harm than snakes.

And should she tease apparent happiness,
know me through her warmth, menace affection,

treat me to it, attention and inflamed touch;
as she will, she may, as she might, and do

tomorrow as did this very afternoon –
rest shoulder minus sleeve on my stopped hand:

perched then there no one thought felt soft remove,
opposed prey prayer, deafen too merciless

insolvent entreaty – set flesh to salt
before hers. I burned on water, like to melt:

a foundered ship taken by exquisite storm.
I never wished to quit that peril –

end, come, must suffer, ever; still preserve, else
such salvages could I perish of its slight.

Last Night

John Jack Cooper

What chance had I to give, what wish grant?
The off-chance all I ever knew —
remained obscure: eclipsed in shadow
by excuse for what never was;

the might that could, the dare that would
not, unable or unknowing how,
never did. We stirred while all else slept.
Undressed in darkness hours seemed

palaces of sense lord blind had fled,
leaving second-best, secondhand bed.
Feathered minutes flew, unleashed our springs,
fed the source velleity forswore,

vacancy substituted for life
uninhabited, waiting, when, compelled
to travel light, I only found time
to long, so short we barely drew breath.

Forgive me! oh forgive my having
valued less us than even my own
self should never have touched, innocent
of love, nor quenched fire without burn.

untitled

Robin Wyatt Dunn

tell me the name of your mother
whose arch and weight
belted boarded and exact
the fact of the matter is that
all this height
strange and new and vast
exacted at the pass for your arrival
bid and beckoned shrewd and fine your immaterial vision
tried troweled and in wine set for the feast upon the wall
all our children:

tell me whose and which
the band of the mark
bereft but solemn for the shrine of our desire
hurtling windward
fine
into the iron

tell me why your belt is mine
tell me why the satellites divine peruse your face
your leather strap your whining trap
the machine of love:

name me the enterprise
name the raptor holy
name me the energy entire
rafting over your head
the alma mater
pia mater
stainless ocean cut for seeds
rackless
roaming under your head

for the life

"WHAT MAKES PEOPLE SICK?"

J. H. Johns

Is it the-
red meat,
fat,
sugar,
cigarettes,
alcohol,
salt,
pollutants,
toxins-

too much of this
and too little of that?

Sure,
I'll buy what they're saying-

but-

only if they include
the hassles, stresses and confusion

of the abysmal-
Kafkaesque-

world of

medical billing!

Return to Kissing

John Bowden

I want to use up all the lines I write and
Planned to use in other places.
Make my fingers speak, as if I needed
Translation, interpretation—

Soft TV glow—night's light answer,
My hands make decisions I can't affect.
Kiss me so I can't go to work on Monday—
And in between I want to hear your voice,

Call my name and I'll call yours back.
Three sweet syllables and we're ready to
Return to kissing—your breath my skin
From the world—verbs collected, sorted, filed.

Kisses ignite the worker in me—
Go ahead! I'm insured, conjured into the
Gift I've always prayed to be.
Such a better fate than wisdom, you know,

A better taste than soul, than forever.
I fall into hard praise, my voice on pitch,
And please, please, more kisses
Than I deserve, than I can stuff into my pockets,

To hold for lonely afternoons—
Or when I need to stop time for you,
To shrink the circle of us,
So we can't ever escape

Darkness
Anwesha Paul

I exist.
Not visible to the eye
Subtler than air
In total silence
And in a deafening stillness
I exist.

I existed before time
And I will exist after it
For I am beyond it.

I exist.
Before the universe came into creation
For all arises from the womb of the void

And yet we fear
This nothingness.
This nothingness which is our mother and our grave.

Hope

Ajanta Paul

Hope is a letter
Delivered in the mailbox
Of the morning
After a long wait.

An envelope with
A smell of the future
Awakening promise
In its manila texture.

Your name scrawled carelessly
On its surface
Brings a smile to your lips,
So you are not forgotten

In fate's cryptic correspondence
As it inscribes its impressions
On the sunbeam of sentience
Sloping away to shadow.

You turn the envelope around
And find it tightly sealed.
Well, no matter,
You don't want it revealed

Just yet,
Let it be a rationed diet
To subsist on
Till the next portion on your plate.

Anthology of Affections

Ajanta Paul

Love is not an entry
In my anthology of affections.
You will not
Find its name
In the table of contents,
Or its mention
In the credits
That follow at the end.

No, not in the items
Included for your eyes,
Not even a footnote
Which takes you by surprise.
Neither in the foreword
To the fraternity of feelings,
Nor in the notes
Which elucidate most things.

You can see it, perhaps
Between the lines
As it shines for a moment
And then is gone.
Or catch its odour,
In the mustiness of old paper,
Perhaps, the rustle of its laugh
As you turn the pages.

Like the silverfish, poring
Over an ancient tome, and boring
Gaps in that which it loves,
Love devours its own sustenance
Till there are no more words to chew on
Or flavor of thought to savour
Save designs of its desire
Disintegrating in a shower of dust.

The Patron Saints

Nicholas Karavatos

The personation
      of
Kristoffer
Kristofferson.

Jai Shri Ram   Tabrez Ansari is tied to a tree and later dies
                                        incommunicado
              in police custody.
              Would Bob *Lonesome Death of Hattie Carrol* Dylan

              have left Sinead O'Conner blowing in the wind, hung
out on a limb had his Birthday Tribute Concert mob strung her up for
[her warrior eyes locked on our camera

lens then she rips in halves the photo of her
infallible Pope] accusing the Catholic Church of covering up child abuse?

Rows of Tudor gallows fill the empty English countryside on Showtime, CBC & BBC
                  TV to enforce the Protestant Reformation of Henry.

Jai Shri Ram   Hafeez Mohd Sakrukh Halder is pushed out of a moving train
                              in Kolkata.
              Bob *Nobel Prize for Literature* Dylan
              abandons O'Conner's freedom bus to the firebomb
                  of Magdalena washout.

Jai Shri Ram   Minority members of parliament heckled by their colleagues
          when they stand to take the oath of office.

    [*Judas!*]   I don't believe you. You're a liar."
          [aside to The Band]   Play fucking loud."

"Once upon a time, you …

[Utilizing the bricks and mortar of cultural appropriation]
excerpt from "Judeophobia"
Nicholas Karavatos

            Utilizing the bricks and mortar of cultural appropriation
the Caliphs would not make the same foundational and organizational errors
as had the individual Apostles of Christ.

One People In One Faith from its founding
                        as had the Hebrew Tribes, not a
vague State stitched into pyramids three semiotic centuries later
                        as had the Christians' Churches.

             One ring to rule us all.
             One authoritative text in one language from day one
more like the Canterbury Tales in Middle English by Chaucer
than the Grimm Brothers in the Germanic
             – multicultural writings, of diverse
Judaism and Christianity – canonical or apocryphal – the otherwise forgotten, remembered
to one twirled yarn
   one authority
   one pathway in one language a Sanskrit God that switched from speaking Hebrew
                    to Arabic because the Jews were [*fill it in*].

The Third Monochrome of Magical Penmanships, the Literati of the Divinely Inspired
must avoid a Council of Ephesus or Nicaea or a
             Council of Chalcedon. The new world must avoid the gnosis of
          a Sufi – mystics and seers are rabble-rousers in Theistic States
               as seen in the Judaic Prophetic Tradition
and Christian monks, isolated
psychedelic drunkards misappropriating sexuality since the Iron Age.

The Jewish Covenant with The Explicit Name is first appropriated by Christianity.
                  is first colonized by Christianity.

The spiritual literature of the Hebrew Tribes
is appropriated as the mythos of diverse Others – and added to by foreign languages.

The Jewish Covenant with The Explicit Name is next appropriated by Islam.
                  is next colonized by Islam.
The emulated cleanliness becomes
a kosher-lite.

The spiritual literature of the Hebrew Tribes and of "Judeo-Christianity"

appropriated as the mythos of diverse Others – envisioned as a single vision
decentered document revised
with local characters in its already stellar cast of classics – but
a pantheon is
a pantheon and we enter ourselves to become the story. When in Rome.

The Most Brazen Wins

Gavin Bourke

The faces, everywhere, every day, closer,
the same lens, different angle, no discernible
end, no memorable beginning, continuous, endless,
greed and avarice, chi-ching, click-a-thons-for a few
million more, each year, to finance, another fleet of
jeeps and cars, scraping the pockets, of the
unsuspecting, cynical moves, pouts and po faces,
over nothing, of any importance, even to commerce,
resulting in insufferable motives and intentions,
to bear witness to, again and again.
The bones, breaking through, the most, shallow and
Base, of objectives, plucked chicken-heads, everything
they do, all for themselves, only, sold themselves, to
pariah-dom, for the coldest, hardest cash, hard to cancel,
the cancelled, facing the bones, each day, until they
chalk themselves, into your dreams and consciousnesses,
individually and collectively, drilling slowly, mining, even
more slowly, like hungry, rabid wolves, gnawing at, your
grey matter, way beyond, banned, subliminal, tales of
yarn and tweed, all the way, to their original, dirt tracks,
insufferable megapixels, despicable necks, of solid brass,
to which, insults and criticisms, are construed as
compliments, as long as, the brass coins, continue,
to stack up, high, leaving you, with the feeling,
of having been fooled, repeatedly, willingly.

I'm Tired

Lynn White

I'm tired of trying to see the good in people.
I'm tired of making decisions about good and bad.
I'm tired of endless discussions in armchairs
judging and justifying what is good or bad.
I'm tired of procrastination,
of enquiries and commissions designed
to delay until death or forgetfulness.
Tired of time servers,
jobs worths,
pocket liners.
Tired of them all.
So where shall I go now?

To Rest In Peace

Lynn White

They were men of the north
suitably suited
in black dense as new hewed coal
or dark grey shiny as wet slate
or, rarely, the midnight blue
of a northern night sky.
It was a formal occasion
this laying to rest
of the dull grey
past known,
of the bright red
future hoped for.
They laid them to rest
with broken flowers
petals crushed
with ashes
and dust.
It was a formal occasion
this laying to rest
in peace
or not.

There was a Lot to Love

Dharmpal Mahendra Jain

There was a lot to love:
morning with the warmth of rays,
birds chirping,
tireless insects hovering
around the blooming flowers.
I was like a drop of dew
on a blade of soft grass,
ever afraid of the wind.
I couldn't learn to fly with it.

There was a lot to love:
lofty mountains chatting with the sky,
piercing through the clouds.
Waterfalls melting the elegance
of every joint of the rocks.
There was a river in the valley,
flowing with great zeal,
making a soft and pleasant sound
and irrigating a huge span of the earth.
I was stuck like a rock at its bottom.
I couldn't learn to merge
and flow with it.

There was a lot to love:
having handed over to nature all they had,
with a passion for decorating themselves
again and again.
There were trees with loads of fruits,
green fields with ears full of corn,
vines blossoming with bountiful flowers.
I stood like a stump,
measuring my height.
I never learned to link roots with the soil.

There was a lot to love:
once you were there on a vagrant evening.
The moonlight was affectionate, clear.
It was a shimmering, silent night.
I was burning like fire, high and low.
I could not learn to come out of myself
and live within you.

There was a lot to love.
I just did not know how to love.

God Left Holding the String

E. Martin Pederson

top flicks out with a bump
leans in, spin
in larger then smaller circles
straightens up
winds down
teeters around one spot
tips and rocks
stops with a whiplash
imperceptibly cradled still hugging itself
to that unique place
where friction buzzes
drawn
by luck
presumably
as I
to all this
dizziness

I Am Weathered

Lindsey Morrison Grant

I awoke in a Tsunami
of words and images
a flood-tide of memories
swept away with the debris
of age and culling of tears
with appreciation for the depth
of my love for you

I awoke in an Earthquake
shattering of notions
and emotions
I'd left on the shelf
of reluctant language
gathering dust on mementos,
the triggers of time machines
and substance of naught

I awoke in a Hurricane
of tumultuous greed
a desire to capture time in a bottle
curry thoughts into understanding
battling the whirlwind of memories
scattered across acres and aches
yardage and years
to make sense of the nonsense

to make love despite pain
to recapture the good
and to stomp in puddles left in its wake
with the childlike joy of a sage

Sitting before Sunset

Lindsey Morrison Grant

The window wide open...
    waves of wondrous weary
        the reward of the day's tasks
           complete
Soothing streams of sunlight
    warm thin skin
        and trigger tears and memory
Too many tasks
    too little time
Sun sets too often
    and too soon
Grasp the moments
    Opportunity's glorious array
meets the awkwardly urgent
    advancing of age
The window wide open...
    title waves of an age
        The reward for Life's tasks
           complete

Annihilation
Freena R.

Walking on rooftops
the city stumbles on a cloud
Its toe, a slum, bleeds down sooty chimneys

In a kitchen, a woman catches fire
She walks in flames into the night
touching every passerby
The man with the fields in his heart
watches the ripe corn turn golden
and explode
The one with a river in his,
sizzles, falling as ash

The city swings through the night
Its feet dangling in cool air
Below it, vacuum sucks the living into a sinkhole

In its graveyard, flowers come alive
Withered bouquets throw out lightning blooms
Sleeping stones move aside to let a procession of crows march underground
A protest against the city's abrupt departure

The city meanwhile, has climbed onto the clouds
It lurches, hands on hips, its massive jaws apart, drooling lava
The airplanes that took off from the airports buzz around, trying to evade a ravenous mouth

The woman, still aflame, climbs out of her skin
She spreads it over the city and the city sleeps

Flirtations

Reena R.

We sit at different tables
our eyes fixated on a weak spot
forgetting to breathe
not wanting to let go
of hands that come through the screen

All around chatter floats and swirls
curling around unwary ankles
gorging
fattening upon flung scraps of rumours

At the fish market
I meditate upon the taste of your words
my buds cringing from the misaligned flavors

Millions of fingers poised upon keys
Millions of desires let loose,
wandering free
mock us through poetry

for though I write a thousand words
I never say one to you
and though you paint desire at her utmost
fiercest, you never touch me

for the grave I want to sink into
and the wounds that are killing you
are at the same depth
but
in different worlds

so our laughter dies
in a sinkhole
and I wear the taunt like a crushed flower
under my sole
writing guarded epistles
while fast forwarding a lifetime
on a slow remote

Mere flirtation
this banter between the vanquished
and the dead

Melancholy

Navneet K. Maun

Melancholy, creeps in suddenly
an uninvited guest
residing in the soul
disturbing the peace of mind.
The zest for life gone.
So was it,
with Antonio
many centuries ago.
Having no inkling
about the nature of his sadness.
Did Alexander The Great
have moments of despair
agonizing in Babylon
his dream unrealized.
Glamour, beauty, stardom
were not enough to sustain
Marilyn Monroe, the diva.
Loneliness eating the vitals of her heart
struggling with addiction, depression.
The malaise increasing disconcertingly
is a matter of concern.
The young generation succumbing
to the pressures of life.
The tidal waves of emotions
washing away sanity.
The rejection, dejection playing havoc.
The fragile mind
crumbling like sand castles
under the gust of wind
unable to accept failure.
The weary, depressed mind
yearning for solace

the eternal sleep.....

Blood

Belinda Subraman

My lip bleeds at night.
I wake up with a wet trickle
sliding down my chin.

Maybe I bite my lip against the onslaught
of exclusion, division, fear
and the unnatural affection for guns.
Arguments and hate
spew on my compassion.

Cargo trains mysteriously rumble
through American deserts
where 1000s have disappeared already.
Women, just for being women.
Land of Indian Holocaust. Japanese internment.
McCarthy era. Slavery.....
It's still happening.

What is America?
A hemisphere, a region, an idea
where God and the flag
are code words
for the final solution?

I bleed for myself
I bleed for humanity.
I bleed because I'm alive.

Hurricane Dandelion

Belinda Subraman

man in holy robes
with little boy breath

biting tone

Isis sex slaves

God, a monster
in a broken mirror

polished air
sands his lungs

wet sand nurses
his feet

his white dough mask
begins to crack
greedy, desperate, scared
knots unwind in his brain
cholesterol bulges his veins
repeating generalities
and irrationalities
his heart explodes

surgeons are burdened

flowers
seed the wind

Clark Coolidge: Maintenance

Stephen Bett

belonging to slow the means day in the period
of a tree a book as by the stretch to right
milk legitimate legs
or of a group long or on side

excerpt from The Maintains — Clark Coolidge

belonging to slow the means day in the period
or of a group long or on side
of a tree a book as by the stretch to right
milk legitimate legs

of a tree a book as by the stretch to right
milk legitimate legs
belonging to slow the means day in the period
or of a group long or on side

milk legitimate legs
or of a group long or on side
of a tree a book as by the stretch to right
belonging to slow the means day in the period

or of a group long or on side
belonging to slow the means day in the period
milk legitimate legs
of a tree a book as by the stretch to right

Philip Whalen: Vernacular Drift

Stephen Bett

I praise those ancient Chinamen
Who left me a few words,
Usually a pointless joke or a silly question
            *   *   *
& konked out among the busted spring rain cherryblossom winejars

Hymnus Ad Patrem Sinensis—Philip Whalen *(with more nods to PW)*

I praise those ancient Chinamen
dose old vernaculars   key is *praise*   so no shoot …
first's the big ask   ahh Zen monk(ery)   lovely man!
bits of sugar-blossom in his beard [1]

Who left me a few words,
a *continuous fabric (nerve movie?)*
Bald and pink and great
This is a man you could love [2]

Usually a pointless joke or a silly question
(*If You're So Smart, Why Ain't You Rich?*)
Anybody (quote) who doesn't love & admire
~~Allen Ginsberg~~ [Philip Whalen] is an asshole [3]

& konked out among the busted spring rain cherryblossom winejars
Zen Cowboys [4] take a load off   *clink   clink   clink   clank   clink*
Sinologists spank ol' Fenollosa, the five character shift [5]
Happy to have saved us all [!]

---

[1] This & other italicized lines from this & other PW poems.
[2] These two lines from Michael Rothenberg's journal poem *Unhurried Vision*, written while MR was caregiver to a bravely dying Philip Whalen. MR's stanza continues, "And the poetry he makes/can jump out the window/and get away fast"
[3] Ed Sanders said this about Ginsberg, in Sanders' novel *Shards of God.*
[4] Dale Smith (of *Skanky Possum* fame) quoting Ron Silliman on Whalen & Dorn.
[5] See "Three characters," in *Lucy Kent & other poems.*

The Shower
A. Whittenberg

It's winter.
The water runs cold
She is about the blizzards
She imagined as a child
How she'd think of herself trapped
And far from home, the spring
With its gentle rain never coming,
Those summers with their nights
Of heat lightning
Court and spark...

Synchronizing
A. Whittenberg

I'm indigent, I think
And you are poignant
In my heart, like an instrument
Are you there to pierce
Or to mend?
Doppelganger emotions
With their fervid, florid intentions
Clutching happiness by its throat
How does the theorem add?
One plus one.
So simple to apprehend, yet hard to apprehend
I never know if I'm fighting
For peace or merely reposing
Between battles
What did Wilde say
Is it who in love is poor or
whoever has love is rich?
There is a difference.

My City and Me(5/5/19)
Dr. Paramita Mukherjee Mullick

I travelled far and wide, I travelled all around.
But I love you the most that's what I found.
Saw rivers, valleys and beautiful scenes.
But came back to you, where long I have been.

My city and me, a relationship of long.
About you my city I have written many a song.
Your skyline with skyscrapers and electric poles.
Your beauty of emotions and love is manifold.

You have pulled me out of many dangers.
I have befriended many strangers.
There are so many problems every day.
My city you have taught me to face them in every way.

The Eternal Feeling
Dr. Paramita Mukherjee Mullick

I am no Coleridge, no Keats, no Shelley.
I am a simple woman; I have no simile.
I write what comes to my mind.
I write about interesting happenings I find.
Don't compare me to Barrett or Browning.
Don't misunderstand my frowning.
These are expressions of a free minded woman.
Free to do things and think without a rein.
I am no Byron, no Wordsworth.
My pen expresses sadness and mirth.
I sing about the beautiful white dove.
I sing about the eternal feeling called love.

Heart of Imroz

Sanket Mhatre

Have you ever measured silence in inches?
From one door to another?
From one end of the balcony to the next?
Ceiling fan to ceiling fan?
A liquid that fills up in these crevices on a Sunday afternoon
When everybody is asleep?
Submerging eyes, who'd just dreamt of a naked sea in Palolem
A wedding festivity;
A final dip into the deep sea with rise on the other side of the continent
Where new truth could be discovered;
Where past is left on the last shores
And there's new present to be written.
But here, on these shores of the dark Mumbai skyline
Which you saw with him and me with her
Arms wrapped around waists like boulders
Hands clutched tightly
When we said – we'll try one more time!
Guilt comes close and plays like a rat on your chest
before biting your finger, in your sleep.
Have you ever clutched vacuum in your hands,
after anybody has abandoned you?
(Do you know how sticky it gets?)
Before you frantically punch words
Hoping your loneliness will pulsate one last time and then disappear
Knowing I could never be hers, before?
Silence is standing with a mad-eye on a remote highway
One step closer to death that approaches like a truck
One step and you'd be the road and nothing else.
Silence is a room with a red bulb
Where the last known riot has dissipated
Knowing this wasn't the only time she was not yours
Silence is making love to this jagged truth
And there's no hand to keep on your chest
No touch that tells you it's just a story
And now there will be no more
Silence could be a cold flower on your naked body
That has missed her and missed her for years
Until you found her in another body
In another room
Of another motel
Quicksilver love,
Quicksand hours,

Quick lump of emptiness, removed temporarily
Silence is finding the symphony of bodies
She might have found earlier
And you denied it to someone else
Silence is knowing how she must have felt
When we both knew we could have had a child together
And we both knew it would be a boy, like her
Silence is standing on the fulcrum of a thousand apologies
Under her window where she doesn't live anymore
Hoping she never forgives you or your lunatic behaviour
In this final silence,
you now have to exchange the heart of Amrita
for the heart of Imroz
Silence is also knowing that this truth will repeat itself
In every poem, after this.
Every time you meet her
Or someone like her

These Years with Her

Sanket Mhatre

Line after line crashes
On the last shores of the soul
Pulling me into her sacramental bosom of unfathomable depth
Wait – her depth isn't depth but a rhythm
That reacts to the words that echo under your skin
Her depth is malleable; Her depth is made of water
No lines are ever written on pages
But spoken to the winds
Or pasted on skies so I could pluck them
And turn them into a poem
A verse could be an open road with her
A verse could lead to mutating rooms of refracted possibilities
A verse could be layers & layers of skin spirally bound by your body
There are no trial jumps with her
But a straight dive into an ocean in tumult
Without any diving cylinders or masks
These years with her are dog-eared
Earned, one poem at a time.

A Parade of Gates

Paul Ilechko

1: mouth as gate

There are so many gates to pass through
                some open   some closed
for example
                      my mouth is a gate

for example
                     all of our mouths are gates
our feet leave traces   in the broken glass
              as we pass from gate to gate

2: glass from ocean

the glass is a mystery   embedded
                  in the soil
between the hyacinths
                       scattered
in small piles of fragments   among
             the rose bushes
the glass is persistent   as the smell
     of ocean   the glass-green ocean

3: other people

I pass through a gate
                that stops me from drinking
I pass through a gate
                that sickens my blood
                and weakens my bones

the people around me are gate-heavy
        they are gate-frazzled
                as they drink and die

4: *ocean and birds*

ocean is a mystery that is lacking borders
                              as fragile bird-life
                                        darts and swoops
                                        between the waves

or stumbles through the surrendered
                                        agitation of sand
                        gates cannot control the motion of birds

5: *power of gate*

I pass through a gate
                                        that allows me to write
I pass through a gate
                                        that requires me
                        to change the way
                                        in which I live my life
some gates are more importunate
                                        than others

6: *triggering*

there are so many gates to pass through
            for example
                                        my speech is a trigger
                                        that opens a gate
for example
                                        my emotion is a trigger
                                        that closes another

my words leave traces in the sand
                        that one day will be smooth
                                                    as glass
            that one day will be expansive
                                        as ocean.

Tessellation

Paul Ilechko

White birds are everywhere   as if
        a mattress detonated   feathers bisect
like entropy in action
            white birds

are snaking over water   long-legged
       and piercing dagger beaks   that skewer
and swallow
            white clouds that fade

through violet to darkness   as
     somewhere north of here   the starlings rise
and circle in the gusty winter winds

  their swirl the swirl of trash in motion
        of smoke   and soot   and tattered squall
of fragments   that seem extracted from

a greater puzzle
           and if they greet white
birds in motion   an Escher tessellation
      fills our world with interlocked enigmas

  but now   we have petrified the world
and bird are staring   one eyed   side
    glancing   and unresolved
            motionless against

the power that we exude   as organizers
      of the space containing them   and we...
we exult in our implausible capacity.

New Cathedral

Paul Ilechko

Whisperings among the rubble
beneath the shadows of the statues

of dead men   and their mighty horses
the broken glass of cathedral windows

the lonely bugle sounds   inside
your head   as the general stands to make

his final speech   and all around the spreading
fields of empty blankness

where fires blazed   and flame-bleached
bones have seeded the land in preparation

for a dreadful harvest   this world become
a blessing in disguise   a time of regeneration

a time of new beginnings   a motherless nation
moving slowly   growing into itself and choosing

finally   choosing life over death   choosing light
over darkness   choosing kindness over hatred

sinking a foundation into the corpse
bloodied ground   and building upwards.

The bear and the brown sahib

Sunil Sharma

Nobody was ready for the latest shock.

A dancing bear had escaped and seen prowling in the posh area, a mix of woods and bungalows, on the central hill overlooking a pale-yellow lake in a haven for those who wanted to escape the madness of Mumbai and live in nature.

The residents were like a joint family in the initial years. The town was small and not on the tourist map. Folks could easily drink in pure air. Trees lined the broad avenues. There were hills around and the terraced cottages added to its primeval appeal to a largely retired population. Few shops catered to their basic needs. It was a laid-back place where time had slowed down and people loved listening to the trees, rains and winds, in their backyards and neighbours stopped and did exchange greetings in the middle of a deserted street. The moon and stars guided the gloomy paths. A clean lake with boats; a bandstand and horse rides; walk on the promenade and no crime---it was heaven.

It turned out to be a short-lived dream!

The town got discovered.

And the innocence was lost.

The builder lobby saw gold in the dust of that hamlet-like place.

Everything changed fast.

The general peace was shattered by the invading machines that flattened the hills and trees within few years. A glitzy hill station was born on the razed forest land.

As it happens in similar boom- narratives, the old charm was gone forever, so was the tranquility, once the sleepy Shangri-La got discovered by the hungry consumers for new experiences.

The tourists made life hell.

The residents bore the brunt of the rapid urbanization of an obscure hill station, now ferociously coveted for its natural beauty and cooler climate. The place enjoyed the financial gains but hated the source of the cash flow: the uncouth travellers. Noise pollution increased. Littering became rampant. The attendant hooliganism by the drunken parties was an additional nuisance. Traffic was a nightmare.

Social divisions widened.

Big-bungalow owners acted as the *pucca* Brown Sahibs---English manners and dress, polo-and-cricket-and-horse-race-obsessed; and, playing bridge, billiards, cards and drinking rum at the Raj Club, with religious fervour.

The Sahibs treated the rest, including the apartment-owners, as the little people, of no importance.

The locals---displaced tribals and marginal farmers---were low class.

Tourists were collectively resented and fights erupted frequently.

It was an uneasy mix. The fault-lines clear and deepening.

The tourist season was mostly unpredictable.

Cops were ready for the heavy rush.

Local businesses expected a windfall.

The Sahibs were secluded in their huge bungalows and avoided the public places.

.

This summer was no different.

The usual hordes had arrived in cars and buses; the hotels, bars and scenic spots swarmed with the noisy packs of loud families, students, young men in groups, solo and some camera-toting *firangi* visitors.

As usual, the residents braced themselves for the long onslaught.

Then, something unexpected happened.

An invisible virus stopped the flow of cash and sightseers. The town went into quarantine due to the fear of the COVID-19.

A killer was on the loose!

A silent slayer.

People went indoors---and remained there only. The lockdown was unprecedented and complete.

The arrogance of humans!

A virus made them bend.

The tourists fled.

Shops shut down.

Roads became empty.

Threat was real for a divided community.

There was an upside to the shutdown also.

The residents were back to the old days of solitude, crisp air, bird songs and no traffic---but imprisoned in homes.

Days and nights grew monotonous, endless and people grew restless but did not stir out, as the enemy was round the corner.

The slide began.

Many small businesses got ruined. Migrant labour returned to their states.

As people remained caged, a fresh threat emerged---of a dancing bear stalking the town.

It further terrified the already-terrified town.

Rumours floated freely.

Shadows became bears.

Reports, unconfirmed, circulated on the social media of the encounters with a grisly giant.

Days grew scary.

Nights, worst.

Practically, everybody had seen the new monster, and, not seen it.

There were conflicting versions---bear; bears; sighted, not sighted. Here. There. Everywhere. Nowhere.

Even the bear-catchers failed to catch the elusive animal.

Its master---a middle-aged Kalandar---had fled.

There was no way of capturing the runaway beast in the lockdown.

Everybody felt doubly vulnerable.

The terror soon began in that small hill station.

.

On quiet nights, the residents started hearing the growls of the beast and lost sleep.

Shangri-La was under the dual siege mentality.

Any unfamiliar sound or scraping of leaves---and the people scampered to their inner rooms and locked themselves firmly inside those tiny dungeons, offering prayers.

The ensuing panic took on the form of a parallel pandemic.

First---Corona.

Now, this four-legged marauder.

No income. Huge losses. Imprisonment.

Death was in the air.

Nobody knew who the next victim was.

Their remote paradise had turned into a stinking hell within 90 days flat!

"What will we do, if he crosses into our courtyard, that ugly bear?"

"Do not worry, honey. I will take care of intruders, human or animal."

The petite woman draped over the sofa purred in a husky tone: "My hero. My saviour."

He replied softly. "For you, anything, my *Jaan*."

She smiled. "Lucky to have married a top marksman. You feel safe with a long-distance shooter with so many trophies."

"Never be afraid, darling! First lesson of shooting."

"But this beast is dangerous. Mauled few residents already."

"Do not worry. Will kill with bare hands anyone who tries to attack my love, my Lily."

She curled up, eyes fluttering, lips pouting and crooned, "Oh! My baby!"

He was smitten. "You are deadlier than the beast."

She gave him a smoky look and murmured, "Come on! I am not a beast."

He smiled: "That style! I ran away with you just for the killer look."

She grinned. "Oh! My parents are very cross with you for kidnapping me."

"So is my wife."

She smiled. "Who cares?"

"They are angry, your parents, because I stole their cash cow. Shameless guys! Surviving on the earnings of their daughter who was a belly dancer in a night club. Now you have got name and wealth."

She said nothing.

"And respect," he said, lighting up.

She did not reply. Only fluttered long eyebrows.

The butler coughed.

"Yes?" He asked.

"Dinner ready, Saab."

The couple ate a sumptuous dinner in a well-lit large room under the glassy gaze of the mounted heads. A soft music played in the background.

For a second, the shooter thought he saw two glowing eyes in the semi-darkness outside an open window. His heart missed a beat and hand-held wine glass remained suspended midair.

Lily did not notice, busy as she was attacking the butter chicken and garlic *naan*.

The moment he returned gaze to the window, only saw the glimmering gloom. Shadow flickering.

He stared hard. Nothing. A strong wind rattled the tiles.

And then, silence of the night, on a sprawling property, upper reaches of a steep hill.

.

Midnight, he was woken up by a growl.

A distinct sound---somewhere, at the back of his rolling farmhouse---that seemed to be calling the hunter in him.

He got up quietly, took his loaded rifle and slipping a leather jacket and night vision, went out into the cold night; his body totally alert, mind calm, eyes focussed.

I will get you, beast!

The growl changed into a chomp and then, woof.

He felt drawn by a mystic force to its origins beyond the hedges, fence and into the woods at the top of the hilly terrain.

A voice pulling the sniper to his next prey.

The moment, the marksman went into the deep woods, a moon came out and clearly guided him through a dirt trail that went up to the summit.

The sky was a stunning combo of the blue and milky-white. A cold wind kissed him on the rough cheeks.

The sound changed into a bawl, then into a whimper.

It came from a clearing.

He entered the small clearing---and another realm!

First time in his life of 45 years, the shooter felt calmed and in a trance. Everything changed dramatically. The light streaming through the boughs was pure silver and soothing, like the first rains after a long spell of dry heat. A river hummed in the background, kind of gentle sonata, created by the waters flowing peacefully under a clear sky. He could feel the presence of the spirits native to the forest that had come alive, each branch and twig animated and full of joy.

It was another space and temporal dimension, experienced first time, by a never-satiated soul, in search of new sensations and adventures. His rifle often cried for blood and he shot wild fowl or in the air---to stop that intense desire to hunt and kill. He had collected many trophies---animal heads and few shields. But the desire for fresh meat drove him into the valley below, along with his servants and hounds, in an open jeep. Then he would clean the fowl and cook in the jungle, assisted by his butler, on open fire.

Rifle made him feel important and powerful. He had a variety of guns and pistols and prided himself on his hunting skills and a family tradition of courting the danger in the wilds. It made his adrenaline rush like nothing else.

This time, it was different.

Everything looked pure and blissful out here, every inch of the forest- floor and canopy bathed in ecstasy of a type indescribable for mortal eyes.

A novel province had opened up for the hunter being led by a force beyond his control.

Listen to the forest! Dad had told him, a teenage boy, being taught the rules of engagement in the jungle by a well-known *shikari*.

The more you listen, the more you learn to survive.

And he was listening.

The animals never attack, unless provoked. Hunt those who are man-eaters!

That was the command of a man, who had changed after hunting man-eaters for more than three decades of his hunting life.

Dad was a *Zamindar*. And loved hunting big cats, initially, for the thrill and then, the man-eating ones. In his last years, he had totally changed---renouncing gun for the camera for shooting the creatures that he called his gentle four-legged friends!

Such a transformation!

You can survive the jungle, my boy but not the civilization!

That was his parting advice.

The recent confinement was most upsetting for an outdoors-man like him but there was no choice.

He remained indoors, played billiards, swam in the pool and drank rum with Lily. Talked to few friends over phone. Afternoons were for playing cards.

---I am very lucky, thanks to my inheritance! Many people have lost jobs and starving. Things are bad due to the pandemic. But I am fortunate!

He told his love. Lily knew this already.

Over the years, he had honed his skills and earned reputation as a sniper. In his ancestral property, hundred miles away, he had set up a shooting range where he practiced daily. Shooting was always his first love.

Here was the time for testing those skills again, this night.

Listen to the animal being stalked---and to be hunted!

Dad reminding from the other side.

He was ready to face the "beast"---and "kill" it.

I will rid the town of a beast gone rogue!

The squeal came from the thicket. He waited. Rifle ready.

The bellow grew into a whimper.

He was *listening*!

The bawling was 500-hundred meters away, near the river now.

He quietly reached the spot, prepared for the beast.

A soft shadow turned into a bear. A bear crying!

It was heart-wrenching sight---an adult sloth bear crying in that desolate area, like a lost child.

He stood rooted to the spot, hugged by the quivering shadows. A wind rising off the milky-white river further cooled his mind and heart.

The bear was weeping loudly now, calling out in bear-language, Mama, mama!

This totally surprised him.

The sloth bear not only could dance but talk also!

Unbelievable!

His heart melted---and strangely, he no longer was fearful of the fully-grown bear that could attack him there.

He dropped his rifle---and approached the sobbing beast, his heart full of love and compassion.

The beast saw him coming but he did not react to the bipedal danger.

---Bear, why crying?

The bear looked up, eyes innocent: Go away human! You have already killed my family, tortured me and almost destroyed my sanity.

---How?

At that precise moment, the shooter saw clearly the reasons for the bear's misery, in his eyes; kind of film rewinding and then being projected on a screen by the same force that had brought him here.

A montage of violent images unspooling:

In the jungle, the poachers killing mama bear and taking away her two wailing kids; selling the lost siblings on the black market; a family of kalanders torturing starving training them as acrobats, one of them dies early in the process; the survivor dancing in small towns and villages for an audience that hardly pays for the performing animal in great pain; the bear finally escaping his tormentor and the catchers; roaming hungry and being attacked, and, coming to the river where he hides in a narrow cave, coming out stealthily and remembering his murdered mother and her ruthless killers with guns and darts and cages...

The extraordinary journey did not stop there.

Another unusual development happened:

It was the sound that did that.

The sniper heard a pack of hounds barking in the dark woods and started changing involuntarily into a bear!!!

As the hounds came, followed by the hunters and drum beaters from behind the thicket of trees into the clearing, the hunter-bear trembled and ran for his life, the hounds and hunters at his heels, trying to corner the prey into a gully. The bullets fly, he flies into the gully and breaks his hind legs. More bullets follow. And these find his heart and lungs, the hail of bullets and stones, and he bleeds to death slowly there, the hunters waiting above...

Then, surprisingly, the scene is restored and he is back talking to a crying bear.

---Sorry bear!

---No need. Want to kill me? Do that. Finish my misery, human.

The marksman stood up, threw down his rifle into the crystal-clear river and said to the bear: I will come back to take you to a better home, your home, where there are no two-legged predators. Go back to your cave, otherwise hunters out there will kill you for the award.

The bear nodded and sprinted down the slope.

.

The shooter did return.

He brought the bear to his huge shooting range converted into a bear park.

He put his collection of guns in his strong room and furry guests behind enclousers where they roamed freely.

He listened to them, the freed bears in that park and attracted media attention.

His popularity arose, as he talked to the bears rescued from their cruel masters and came to be known as the brown sahib who had transformed into a bear listener!

Made in the USA
Middletown, DE
19 April 2021

37902900R10031